·S·H·A·R·K·S·

DESIGNED BY PHILIP CLUCAS
EDITED BY BARRY VARNEY
PRODUCTION: RUTH ARTHUR, DAVID PROFFIT, SALLY CONNOLLY
DIRECTOR OF PUBLISHING: DAVID GIBBON
DIRECTOR OF PRODUCTION: GERALD HUGHES

For Gonzalo

Grateful thanks to Professor Sam H. Gruber for his invaluable comments on the text.

CLB 2356
All photographs drawn from the files of Planet Earth Pictures Ltd.
This edition published in the United States 1990 by Gallery Books
An imprint of W.H. Smith Publishers, Inc.
112 Madison Avenue, New York, New York 10016
© 1990 Colour Library Books Ltd., Godalming, Surrey, England.
Printed and bound in Hong Kong by Leefung Asco Printers Ltd.
All rights reserved.
ISBN 0 8317 7764 8

Gallery Books are available for bulk purchase for sales
promotions and premium use. For details write or telephone
the Manager of Special Sales, W.H. Smith Publishers, Inc.
112 Madison Avenue, New York, New York 10016. (212) 532-6600.

·S·H·A·R·K·S·

·TERESA·FARINO·

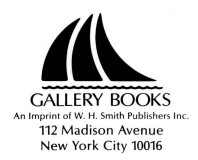

GALLERY BOOKS
An Imprint of W. H. Smith Publishers Inc.
112 Madison Avenue
New York City 10016

olfactory lamellae are situated very close to the large and highly developed olfactory lobe of the forebrain, thus minimizing the time interval between the stimulus and its detection by the shark. Experiments have shown that sharks are able to detect one part of human blood in 10 million parts of sea water; this olfactory sensitivity is thought to be enhanced even further in starving individuals.

When a shark scents something interesting in the water it will automatically turn towards the source; that is, in the direction of the prevailing current. As each nostril alternately receives the stronger stimulus, the shark describes a sinuous course along the scent trail. It is thought that the greater the distance between the nostrils, the more efficiently the shark is able to pinpoint the source; hammerheads, with their nostrils at the extremities of "hammer," are thought to be especially adept in this respect.

All sharks possess paired inner ears which are connected to the outside world by tiny ducts. Resembling the inner ears of most vertebrates, each is composed of two large sacs, the sacculus and the utriculus, off which open three semicircular canals. These three canals lie on different planes: two vertical and at right angles to each other, the third horizontal. At the base of each canal lies a swelling called the ampulla, housing sense organs that respond to the direction of gravity, thus allowing the shark to maintain its upright position in the water. Sound, which is detected as particle displacement, is picked up by sensory organs in the sacculus which contain hair cells. Different shark species are sensitive to different ranges of such "sounds," the most predatory species probably having the widest range. Lemon sharks, for example, respond to vibrations between 100 and 1,500 Hertz, which is about equivalent to the mid-range of human hearing.

Similar cells to those in the sacculus are found in the lateral line system, which consists of subcutaneous canals filled with a gelatinous fluid running along each side of the shark's body and branching around the head. These sensory receptors are able to pick up particle displacement caused by the movements of other creatures, or those created by the shark itself as it approaches a stationary object. The lateral line system has been described as the shark's sense of "distant touch."

Sound travels farther and faster in water than on land; sharks are attracted to irregular, low frequency vibrations, particularly those of less than 40 Hertz at distances of up to about 330 feet. There is speculation that these low frequency waves, typical of the vibrations produced by a wounded fish, are picked up by the lateral line, whereas higher frequencies are detected by the acoustic system.

Although sharks have long been regarded as creatures with poor sight, research carried out between 1960 and 1975 has proved that this is not the case. A shark's eye is not unlike that of higher vertebrates, including man, although the lens is rather more rigid. Most sharks have both rods and cones in the retina, which theoretically means that they should be able to detect differences in color; they have been shown to be particularly sensitive to contrasts between light and dark. The most predatory sharks, such as carcharhinids and threshers, are thought to excel in the detection of moving objects, even in dim light. The lemon shark, for example, although very far-sighted, has been shown to possess a slightly greater sensitivity to light than man.

Perhaps the most interesting feature of the shark's eye is the tapetum lucidum, consisting of a series of silvery plates located behind the retina. In dim conditions, light which has already passed through the eye is reflected back by this mirror-like layer, thus increasing the sensitivity of the retina. In bright light, however, in order to protect the retina from overexposure, a layer of pigmented cells called melanoblasts spreads over the plates of the tapetum lucidum, thus reducing the reflection. Some deep-sea sharks, because they live in perpetual twilight, lack these melanic "sunglasses" and the tapetum lucidum is exposed at all times. This is detected as a luminous greenish shine in the eyes of such creatures when they are hauled to the surface, similar to that seen in the eyes of a cat caught in car headlights.

Owing to prominent eye muscles, sharks are able to maintain an almost panoramic visual field, even when twisting and turning. Some species have fixed eyelids, in some sharks they are mobile, while four families also have a third eyelid, or nictitating membrane. In all cases these function as physical shields, to protect the eyes from damage rather than to control the amount of light entering.

In addition to a keen sense of smell, good auditory perception and reasonable eyesight, sharks have also been recently proved to have a higher sensitivity to electrical stimuli than any other animal ever studied. In a classic set of experiments, small spotted catsharks were shown to be capable of detecting an electric field as low as 0.01 microvolts percentimetre: more than 25 million times weaker than the faintest that man can perceive, and less even than the electrical charge produced by the nerves of a living organism.

Electroreception, as this ability has been called, is probably accomplished by isolated sensory cells known as the ampullae of Lorenzini, which are located on the underside of the shark's snout, although the exact manner in which they function has yet to be ascertained. This acute sensitivity to electric fields is extremely useful to the shark in detecting prey at close range. Sharks have been shown unerringly to locate flounders buried beneath the sand. On the other hand, divers in shark cages attest to the fact that a shark initially attracted to flesh bait will often mistakenly bite at the cage rather than the bait at the last minute, possibly because of the strong galvanic current or corrosion current – a type of electrical field – produced by the metal in sea water.

Some researchers (Gruber and Kalmijn) have recently demonstrated that sharks are even able to utilize their electroreceptive abilities to detect the weak electric fields generated by the ocean currents flowing through the earth's magnetic field, using such information to orient themselves in the open sea, for navigation and for migration over long distances.

Members of the Orectiolobiformes, most sawsharks and some false catsharks have barbels at the front of the head which may be used to "taste" the sea bed in search of suitable quarry, although some workers maintain that these are purely tactile organs. In addition, most sharks have taste buds on the floor of the mouth, the tongue and the pharynx, which are used as a final test as to the edibility or otherwise of their prey.

To locate suitable prey, therefore, sharks are equipped with a more than adequate array of senses. In a typical predatory shark, olfactory and auditory stimuli, which may be detected at a range of hundreds of yards, are thought to provoke exploratory behaviour. A shark following a scent trail or low frequency vibrations will eventually come within visual range of its quarry, although even in the clearest water it seems that about 65 feet is the maximum distance.

It seems that certain movements, such as those produced by a wounded fish, in addition to the strong olfactory and auditory signals which it is now receiving, will stimulate the shark to attack. As the shark closes on its victim, the eyes either roll back in the sockets, as in the case of the great white, or the nictitating membrane covers the eye, as in the requiem sharks, to protect it from any possible damage during the encounter. The shark is now attacking blind, and it is thought that the ampullae of Lorenzini are responsible for guiding it during these crucial last moments. The ultimate test is that of taste; an unpalatable object may be bitten, but is often rejected.

A long-reported characteristic of many observations on shark feeding habits is that of the so-called feeding frenzy. This occurs where many sharks are attracted to the same prey, and possibly as the result of sensory "overload." Some workers suggest feeding frenzies are caused by the powerful vibrations produced by the head-shaking actions of the first shark to feed; others maintain that the stimulus is largely olfactory, provoked by a sudden increase of the concentration of blood in the water. What is certain is that the frenzy does not commence until the prey has been attacked at least once.

Shark senses are not only used in detecting prey and navigation, but are in all probability also employed in finding a mate, for the all-important process of reproduction.

Among some species of shark, especially the carcharhinids, there is a marked tendency for sexually mature individuals to segregate by sex. Males and females are rarely seen in the same area except during the mating season. In some species, especially those with a formidable jaw armature, it is thought that the males develop an inhibition to feeding at the onset of the mating season, possibly to protect the females from any cannibalistic tendencies. Once courtship and copulation have been accomplished, the sexes again separate and the males resume feeding.

Gravid females are also believed to stop feeding as the time of birth approaches, again to avoid the temptation of cannibalism. In many carcharhinid sharks the birth takes place in specific nursery grounds, usually in warm, shallow waters, which must be outside the normal geographical range or preferred habitat of the sexually mature males of the species. The females remain only long enough to give birth and resume feeding after their departure.

Male sharks are easily distinguished from female sharks, even at a glance, by the presence of trailing appendages known as claspers in the region of the pelvic fins. Claspers are elaborate structures with their own complicated muscles, skeleton and innervation, the inner edges of which have rolled up and overlapped to form a groove or tube. The structure is very variable, being more or less flattened or cylindrical, smooth or covered with denticles to act as holdfasts during copulation, according to the species.

Female sharks have two ovaries which are located close to the mouths of a pair of oviducts, although they are not directly connected. Even if only one ovary is functional, therefore, which is the case in a number of shark species, both oviducts are able to receive eggs.

Sharks also display what are known as secondary sexual differences, that is, those which are not directly connected with reproduction. In many species, the female is markedly larger than the male; male bigeye houndsharks, for example, are on average only two-thirds the length of the female and may weigh only one-sixth as much. In the African spotted catshark, however, the male is considerably larger than the female, while male porbeagles average 8.5 feet and females only 7 feet, although this is a rare phenomenon.

Male sharks often have much longer teeth than females of the same species in order to grasp her more firmly during courtship. This is seen in dogfish of the genus *Daenia*, in which the teeth of the males are much more erect, while mature male narrowmouth and redspotted catsharks have longer teeth with fewer cusps than the females. Such sexual dimorphism with respect to dentition is also seen in the barbeled houndshark and the bigeye thresher, although perhaps the most extreme example is that of the broadgill catshark, in which the teeth of the male are more than twice the length and take the form of a single conical cusp, as opposed to the short, three-to five-cusped teeth of the female.

In species which display these dental variations between sexes, the skin of the female is generally much thicker in the region where the male may grasp her during courtship; female blue sharks, for example, have hides up to twice as thick as those of the male, a phenomenon also seen in the barbeled houndshark.

Owing to the difficulties associated with studying shark behaviour in the wild, our knowledge of their courtship and copulation is extremely patchy. In smallspotted catsharks which have been observed mating in captivity, the slender-bodied male is able to wind himself completely around the female, which remains immobile in the normal swimming position. The larger sharks, however, are unable to copulate in this way, since their bodies are far less flexible, a side-by-side approach having been observed in nurse, sand tiger and bamboo sharks.

Fertilization is internal in all sharks, the male inserting first one clasper, then the other, into the cloaca and oviducts of the female. A seawater pump system flushes sperm into the female's cloaca.

Some sharks exhibit delayed fertilization. The female blue shark, for example, can store sperm for months after insemination, waiting for the eggs to mature before fertilization takes place. In other species, such as the basking shark, the spermatozoa are moulded into thin-coated packets known as spermatophores before insertion into the female. As such they are more easily stored by the female shark, the thin coating dissolved only when the sperm are needed to fertilize the eggs.

Young sharks develop by one of three different strategies, although in all cases the eggs, after fertilization, are passed through the shell gland, where they are enclosed within a protective case.

In oviparous species, such as the hornsharks, wobbegongs and most of the catsharks, the cases are thick and leathery; these eggs are discharged from the female, usually in pairs, almost immediately. The most common shape is more or less rectangular, with long sticky tendrils at the corners for secure attachment to corals or rocks. The dimensions and shape of the egg-case and the length of the tendrils vary considerably, however, and are usually species-specific. Swellshark embryos take almost a year to develop, breathing by means of external gills in the meantime. Fullterm swellsharks possess two rows of sharp, backward-pointing denticles on the dorsal surface which are thought to help them to rupture the egg case and aid them in wriggling out of the small opening. These denticles are shed soon after hatching.

The hornsharks, however, produce extraordinary screwlike egg-cases, between 5 and 6 inches in length, with broad lateral flanges and tendrils up to 6.5 feet long extending from the tip. Female Port Jackson sharks have been observed carrying these egg-cases in their mouths and depositing them firmly in rock crevices, where the rubbery shells harden, making the eggs almost impossible to remove, and thus safe from predation The embryo within is nurtured for almost a year by the yolk-sac before it finally emerges.

Viviparous species, such as some houndsharks and most carcharhinids, including bull sharks, blue sharks and the hammerheads, have developed a highly sophisticated method of nurturing their young. The eggs hatch in the oviduct and the yolk-sac of each embryo develops into a placenta in close contact with the uterine wall. The embryo is connected to the placenta by an umbilical cord, through which oxygen and nutrients derived from the blood of the mother are conveyed to the young shark. This is not unlike the reproductive strategy practised by mammals, the most advanced creatures on earth's evolutionary scale.

Ovoviviparous species, which account for the majority of living sharks, produce eggs in thin-walled cases which hatch within the uterus. Here the developing embryos are nourished by huge yolk-sacs and the pups are not released until they are capable of fending for themselves. Most of the Lamniform sharks are thought to conform to this reproductive system, as well as some carcharhinids. No placental connection is formed, but some species may be nourished by a secretion from the lining of the uterus known appropriately as "uterine milk."

Another curious feature of some ovoviviparous species is known as intrauterine cannibalism. Female sand tigers are known to produce large numbers of pea-sized eggs. Following fertilization several eggs in each oviduct hatch, but the most aggressive embryo then proceeds to devour its siblings. The female continues to ovulate to provide food for the developing shark pup, which is born when it attains a length of about 29 inches. A similar phenomenon is thought to occur in threshers, makos, the porbeagle and the salmon shark, although in these species between one and six embryos hatch, feeding on the steady stream of eggs produced by the mother. A 16-foot female thresher may give birth to between one and six pups each measuring an incredible 47 inches, although half of this is tail, and well able to fend for itself in the outside world.

The fact remains that we are remarkably ill-informed as to the reproductive details of most shark species. Since only a single gravid great white shark has been caught to date, much has yet to be learned regarding litter size and the proportions of the pups at birth, although it is thought that, like most lamniform sharks, litters rarely exceed four pups, each around 23 inches in length. Similarly gravid basking sharks have never been encountered, despite the fact that this is a species which is commonly exploited for its large liver.

There is also considerable controversy surrounding the whale shark's method of reproduction. In 1953 in the Gulf of Mexico, a single egg-case was found containing an almost fullterm embryo: a 14 inches replica of the world's largest fish, right down to the checkerboard pattern. More recently, however, young whale sharks have been caught which show distinct umbilical scars, suggesting that vivipary is the normal state of affairs, and that the egg-case was a freak.

In ovoviviparous and viviparous species the young sharks are usually born tail-first, although young hammerheads are delivered headfirst, with the pliable winglike extensions of the head folded back. The enlarged denticles which line the edges of the sawshark pup's elongated rostrum are soft at birth, so as not to damage the mother and the sharp dorsal spines of the spiny dogfish pups are capped with knobs of cartilage for the same reason, these being shed soon after birth.

Shark pups are not born until they are capable of fending for themselves; there are no known instances of postnatal parental care. The gestation period varies greatly between species, that of the tope or school shark being one of the shortest known, at around six months. By contrast, the gestation period of the spiny dogfish is one of the longest known for any vertebrate, the development of the pups sometimes extending over two years. There is some evidence that the gestation period of the basking shark may be even longer, but further research is necessary.

The number of young produced varies from species to species, but litters rarely exceed 100 pups and are usually much smaller. The size of the pups is not necessarily correlated to the size of the parent, or even to the maximum size to which the species may grow. Generally speaking, however, pups which are large in proportion to their mother are few in number per litter.

Information is available for only a few sharks species, generally those that are exploited in some way commercially, or favoured by game fishermen. Most viviparous sharks bear between six and twelve young, although hammerheads commonly produce litters of up to 40. Other species with large litters include the tiger shark, in which sixty or more pups are produced, each measuring around 23 inches, and blue sharks, in which an average of 70 pups each measuring around 17 inches. A 16-foot female bluntnose sixgill shark may produce up to 100 pups, each between 23 and 27 inches long.

Despite man's primeval fear of being eaten alive, which has been exploited with great financial success by the film industry, every year only around 100 reports are received of people being attacked by sharks. Detailed studies of these attacks over a number of years has revealed that the great majority of shark attacks take place in water which is at more than 68°F and more than half within 200 feet of the shore or at the surface of the water. Of course, as we have seen, there are species such as the tiger shark which specifically prefer such warm, shallow waters, but the statistics also indicate very accurately the conditions under which most people are in the water: close to the beach and in the summer in temperate regions or all year round in the tropics.

Fewer than 20 percent of all known shark species have been directly implicated in, or are suspected of, attacks on humans. The most dangerous species by far are the great white, tiger, nurse and bull sharks. The oceanic whitetip is also highly suspect, especially in instances where large numbers of people find themselves in the water after accidents on the high seas. About twenty other species have also been known to attack humans, including sand tigers, Pacific and Atlantic angelsharks, makos, blue and lemon sharks and spotted and tasselled wobbegongs, although most of these are unaggressive species unless provoked. In addition, the colossal basking and whale sharks may inadvertently endanger human life by ramming boats.

Why do sharks attack humans? Various motives have been suggested, including sexual aggression and defense of territories, although, with respect to the latter, sharks defend a moving personal space rather than a fixed geographical point. Extremely high levels of testosterone have been detected in bull and Caribbean reef sharks during the breeding season, which in all probability make them particularly aggressive. Silky sharks and grey reef sharks have recently been shown to possess a complicated range of threat postures, usually involving an arched back, raised snout and lowered tail and pectoral fins, which may relate to space intrusion. These postures are undoubtedly recognized by other sharks as danger signals, which consequently back off, although divers are unlikely to perceive the significance of such actions and may suffer an attack as a result.

A more common motive is undoubtedly the instinctive search for food which takes up much of the shark's time. Sharks have been present on this earth for eons, whereas man's occupation of the planet is by comparison very recent, thus it is not possible that sharks could have evolved specifically to take advantage of man as a prey item. It is commonly believed today that a shark attack on a human being is a case of mistaken identity.

Each year about 15 people are attacked by great white sharks; some two-thirds of the victims subsequently die. Great whites are among the few sharks that regularly prey on marine mammals, especially seals. One theory is that divers and bathers present an aspect not unlike that of an abnormal, clumsy seal in general outline and actions, and since most predators are programmed to instinctively seek out wounded or sick animals, it is not perhaps surprising that sharks are stimulated to attack.

However, the fact remains that, even among habitual swimmers in areas of high risk such as Australia and South Africa, the probability of being attacked by a shark is very low. It has been estimated that the risk of drowning near a bathing beach is over 1,000 times greater than the probability of being the victim of a shark's miscalculation. If these figures are not reassuring enough, the option is to stay out of the water. There are to date no records of sharks attacking humans on dry land!

To look at it from another point of view, far more sharks are dispatched by humans every year than vice versa. The world's commercial catch of sharks, skates and rays currently exceeds 600,000 tons per year, while in the United States the shark fishing industry grosses over $5 million per year, with carcharhinids (37,500 tons per year) and spiny dogfishes (42,000 tons per year) accounting for the majority of catches.

What are these sharks used for? Basking sharks, with their surface-feeding habits and large bulk, once occupied a prominent place in the world's shark fishing industry, although today carcharhinids and squalids are more important. Virtually no part of this gargantuan beast goes to waste. An average-sized basking shark will yield around a ton of pinkish, boneless meat while its liver generates up to 900 litres of oil. The fins are removed for the preparation of shark-fin soup, the flesh is smoked, fried, or minced for use in fishburgers and the skeleton is baked in a huge oven and later ground up for animal feed and fertilizer. But it is the liver-oil of this and other sharks which has the greatest worth.

Until the 1950s shark-liver oil was valued as a major source of vitamin A, although the advent of a cheaper synthetic alternative has today rendered this industry more or less obsolete. Shark-liver oil was also once used to lubricate fine machinery, and although synthetic substitutes are now available there is still little to beat the shark-derived product at high altitudes. The liver of deep-sea sharks is also rich in an oil known as squalene, which is widely used in the cosmetics industry as a skin softener and protector. In addition, the Japanese consider squalene to be a cure for everything from cancer to heart attacks; it is marketed as small capsules known as "marine gold," which sell at around 1,500 dollars per kilogram.

Although in Asian and South Sea Island communities shark meat has always formed a large part of the dietary protein, it is only recently, with the growing need to feed the burgeoning world population, that sharks are becoming widely used as a food species in the western world. Today porbeagles are popular in Italy, catsharks in France, makos and threshers in California and blacktips in Florida, while in Britain more than 12,000 tons of spiny dogfish are landed annually to supply the demands of the fish and chip trade, and sold under the pseudonym of "rock salmon" or "flake."

Other uses of shark products include the manufacture of wallets, handbags and belts from the strong leather produced by tanning the hide. The untanned skin, complete with denticles, was once highly valued among cabinet-makers as a type of sandpaper known as shagreen, and is still used today for samurai sword hilts. Thousands of dogfish find their way onto the dissecting table every year, thus assisting in the training of zoology students the world over. In primitive societies shark teeth have long been used as tools and weapons, while today they are highly valued as jewellery and ornaments in the western world. A tooth of a great white shark, for example, may fetch up to $200 if mounted as a pendant, while a full set of jaws from a large specimen is currently worth up to 7,000 dollars in Australia.

Some of the larger sharks are regarded as exceptional sport by game fishermen. Of particular value are species such as makos, which leap from the water in an attempt to rid themselves of the line, while the prestige associated with single-handedly hauling a large great white from the water is eagerly sought by some fishermen. In recent years the increase in popularity of such sports is having a considerable impact on shark numbers. In 1965, only 2,600 tons of pelagic sharks were landed by game fishermen in the western Atlantic, a figure which had increased to a phenomenal 15,900 tons by 1980.

Current medical opinion is that sharks may have a lot to offer. It has recently been discovered that sharks rarely get cancer and tests have shown that their cartilage contains substances which inhibit the development of tumours implanted in laboratory animals. Another component of shark cartilage, known as chondroiten, has been tested for the manufacture of artificial skin for burn patients and shark corneas have been used to replace damaged corneas in human eyes. In addition, the liver-oil contains a substance known as co-enzyme Q10, which may also have anti-carcinogenic properties.

Sharks have recently come into their own as the star attractions of diving tours, especially in island cultures where tourism is the main source of income. In addition they are also popular with aquaria; with the increase in knowledge of shark biology, many species now survive in captivity. A favourite species with the public is the sand tiger, whose mouth literally bristles with teeth. Up to 15,000 people a day visit the Shark Encounter Tank at Sea World, Florida, where several species of shark can be viewed from a glass-enclosed conveyor belt which passes through the middle of the aquarium.

Sharks are among the most successful of all underwater predators. They are situated at the top of the ocean food chain and as such have few natural enemies other than a larger shark and a wide range of parasites. In all ecosystems, both terrestrial and aquatic, such so-called "apex predators" are present in small numbers as compared to the numbers of organisms at lower levels in the food chain. For example, it is estimated that for every 100,000 sharks taken by the Florida fishery, only 27 are great whites, while between 1957 and 1983, a paltry 76 great whites were caught in the western Atlantic.

An additional problem is that even the smallest shark species reproduce very slowly. As an example, male spiny dogfish do not become sexually mature until about 11 years old, while the females reach breeding age at an incredible 19 or 20 years. Their litters are small, ranging on average between four and seven pups and the gestation period may last up to two years. Although these small sharks are thought to live for anything up to a century, it is clear that overfished populations could take decades to recover, if at all.

In recent years the increased demand for food to support the burgeoning human population has led to the expansion of shark fisheries, although the Food and Agriculture Organization considers only about 7% of shark species to be of major importance commercially. In 1975, California's commercial fisheries landed less than half a million tons of sharks, a figure which had increased sevenfold by 1985.

Unfortunately, examples of the commercial overexploitation of sharks already exist. Achill Island, off the west coast of Ireland, was the site of a thriving industry based on basking sharks in the 1950s and 1960s, up to 1,500 of these colossal fish being taken annually as they cruised close to the shore in the breeding season. A gradual reduction in numbers during the 1970s caused no undue alarm, but today the industry has ground to a complete halt. The local basking shark population has been completely wiped out.

Notwithstanding this poignant example of overfishing, the annual harvest of basking sharks in European waters is still almost certainly exceeding the reproductive capacity of this species. In 1979 fishermen of the European Community and Norway slaughtered 2,266 basking sharks, but in 1986 only 493 were taken. Of those taken females outnumbered males by a ratio of 30 or 40 to one, and most showed signs of recent sexual activity. Thus not only is the current population being threatened, but the next as well.

In Australian waters game fishing is taking its toll on the large, predatory species which confer the greatest kudos among aficionados of the sport. It is suggested that almost half of the sexually mature female great whites have been lost during the past five years. Despite the fact that South Australian waters, particularly the region known as Dangerous Reef, contain a higher concentration of great whites than anywhere else in the world, the 200 or so killed in the past 40 years has put a considerable strain on the population. Scientists and local fishermen alike consider that the presence of 40 great whites in the area is an optimistic estimate and that even if the species was completely protected, recovery would be a slow process.

In attempts to counter the possibility of shark attack, beaches in high risk areas such as southeast Australia and the Natal coast of South Africa have been divided from the open sea by overlapping, weighted gill nets positioned parallel to the shore. Since sharks are unable to swim backwards, once trapped in these nets they rapidly drown; the nets must be inspected regularly for damage, and their cargo of dead sharks extracted. The price paid for such shark-free bathing, however, is high. Statistics over sixteen years pertaining to the Queensland nets make depressing reading. Not only did these nets trap over 20,500 sharks, including many species which are not remotely dangerous to man, but 465 dugongs, 317 porpoises, 2,654 sea turtles and 10,889 rays also became entangled and died.

Sharks have long suffered from poor public relations in the world of man, but at last they are beginning to find friends among their two-legged cohabitants of this planet. The barbaric slaughter of over 100,000 carcharhinid sharks off the coast of Florida earlier this year, when the fins were sliced from the living fish and the worthless remains cast back into the sea to die a slow and agonizing death, provoked a howl of outrage among the general public. Endangered shark species are slowly finding their way onto lists of animals protected by international legislation. The plight of the great white, for example, is considered to be so aggravated by the trade in souvenirs, that it has been proposed for inclusion on Appendix 1 of the Convention on International Trade in Endangered Species of Wild Fauna and Flora (CITES), whereby trade in any part of this shark would be prohibited.

Sharks have occupied the seas of the world for close to 400 million years. For much of this time these graceful yet death-dealing fish ruled supreme in their undersea kingdom, but as man has come to dominate the planet they have suffered increasingly from the invasion of their domain. Supertankers and submarines now traverse wide expanses of ocean previously inhabited only by organic life, large sharks are relentlessly persecuted so that man can immerse himself in the warm coastal seas for pleasure and the oceans are increasingly coming to resemble the sewers of the world as we rid ourselves of the unwanted byproducts of human "civilization."

Aside from the ethical question as to our right to annihilate our fellow species on this planet, if we exterminate the shark, either inadvertently or by design, who knows in what way we might disastrously alter the natural ecological balance of the seas.

The policy of protecting Sydney's beaches with offshore shark nets has been in successful operation for more than fifty years. However, in some areas, such as nearby Botany Bay, the enormous expense of establishing and maintaining similar defenses makes them unfeasible and the authorities can do little more than warn prospective swimmers and divers of the risks of taking to the water (above).

The great white shark (right), owing to its impressive array of gleaming white, razor-sharp teeth, has been elevated to star status by the horror film industry. Although a voracious predator, the great white's reputation as an indiscriminate man-eater is largely unjustified; it is merely doing what Nature intended, in much the same way as the lion, pre-eminent carnivore of the African savanna, does.

A tried and tested way of attracting sharks to a particular area is a process known as 'chumming'. The bait varies greatly, from chopped-up mackerel to slaughterhouse blood and offal. The rapidity with which sharks, in this case a great white accompanied by a host of small bony fish, appear is testimony to their enhanced olfactory senses.

Despite having been the victim of a horrific attack by a great white shark, Australian diver Rodney Fox today dedicates much of his time to the conservation of the species, which is rapidly disappearing from South Australian waters. Trophy-hunting game fishermen are largely to blame for this decline, especially as a set of jaws can fetch as much as 4,000 dollars on the open market.

The great white shark (left) occurs in all tropical, subtropical and temperate seas, including the Mediterranean. It usually frequents relatively shallow offshore waters, although its range extends from the surf line of shallow bays to depths in excess of 3,900 feet.

Although its natural prey also includes bony fish, squid, dolphins and other sharks, the great white has a noted predilection for seals and sealions. A floating dummy attracting the attention of a great white (above) lends weight to the theory that the silhouette of a swimmer or diver resembles that of the shark's favourite pinniped prey.

The mako shark is a solitary, open-ocean
species found in temperate and tropical seas
around the world. One of the fastest of all
fish, it is also capable of making prodigious
leaps clean out of the water, and is thus
greatly prized by game fishermen. Note the
parasitic copepods, with trailing egg-strings,
on the dorsal fin of the above specimen.

Makos, which attain a maximum length of
between ten and thirteen feet, have the
narrow, hooked teeth characteristic of those
sharks that feed predominantly on fish. As
in other mackerel sharks, the upper and
lower lobe of the tail fin are almost equal.
'Mako' is the Maori word for shark.

The sand tiger, also known as the gray nurse
or spotted raggedtooth shark, is a stout-
bodied species found in the Atlantic, Indian
and west Pacific Oceans where it favors
shallow water. Like the mako it is a fish-
eating shark, as its protruding, spike-like
teeth indicate.

Gray reef sharks have the small round eyes
and underslung mouths characteristic of
requiem sharks. Mature specimens are
usually around six feet long, although
individuals of around eight feet are not
unknown.

GRAY REEF SHARK

Although gray reef sharks are usually found in loose aggregations of between twenty and thirty individuals either where reefs drop off into the open ocean or near the ocean floor, solitary individuals are more common in the shallow waters over coral reefs and in lagoons.

The behavior of the gray reef shark is actually better documented than its general biology. When the shark is intimidated, it performs a series of 'threat postures', in which the back is arched, the snout raised and the pectoral fins lowered. If the intimidator does not take heed, it may be pursued and attacked.

Some coral reef localities, such as those around the Maldives in the Indian Ocean, are becoming increasingly popular as places where visiting divers can 'feed' gray reef sharks.

Rarely found close to the shore, the oceanic whitetip is not normally considered a dangerous species, although it is often first on the scene after an accident on the high seas and has been implicated in attacks on survivors in these situations. Oceanic whitetips are identified by the prominent, white-mottled tips to their fins, including the huge, rounded first dorsal.

Although such fast-swimming bony fish as marlin, barracuda and tuna commonly feature in its diet, the oceanic whitetip is considered to be a lazy species, hunting by guile rather than in prolonged bursts of speed. The whitetip is also known to feed on seabirds, marine turtles, mammalian carrion and garbage.

BLACKTIP REEF SHARK

The blacktip reef shark is a small, rather
slender fish distinguished by and named
after its black-tipped fins and tail. It
frequents coral reefs and shallow lagoons in
the Indian and west Pacific Oceans.
Interestingly, it has increased its range to
include the eastern Mediterranean since the
construction of the Suez Canal.

Blacktip reef sharks have narrow-cusped teeth, ideal for a diet that includes small sharks, bony fish and octopus. Blacktips reach a maximum length of about six and a half feet and are considered to be nonaggressive to man.

The Caribbean reef shark occurs in the
shallow inshore waters of both the west
Atlantic Ocean and, as its name suggests,
the Caribbean Sea, especially around the
coral reefs of the West Indies. Tagging the
dorsal fin enables researchers to monitor the
shark's migration patterns using capture-
recapture techniques.

Caribbean reef sharks attain a maximum length of around ten feet and are known to have been involved in several attacks on divers. They are not infrequently encountered lying motionless on the sea floor or in underwater caves, in total contradiction to the old belief that sharks must swim perpetually to obtain oxygen, or die.

Tiger sharks, like Caribbean reef sharks, have been found in a torpid state in underwater caves. It has been suggested that highly oxygenated freshwater currents peculiar to these caves may help to rid the sharks of external marine parasites. Tiger sharks possess the spiracles that are characteristic of true benthic sharks and through which a current of water can be drawn to oxygenate the gills while the shark lies motionless on the bottom.

The tiger shark is second only to the great white in size, in voracity and in its reputation for attacking man. Individuals of over sixteen feet are common. The characteristic vertical stripes from which the species gets its name are only well developed in young sharks and fade in individuals over ten feet.

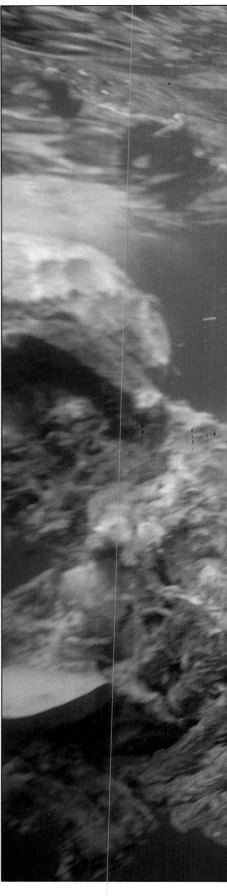

The tiger shark is probably the most opportunistic feeder of all sharks. As it feeds on a whale carcass, the tiger shark churns up the surrounding water with violent sideways movements of its tail and the rear part of its body. These movements are necessary to move the shark's jaws in a sawlike manner through the flesh, thus enabling it to detach a mouthful.

The University of Miami has long been
engaged in studying sharks in their natural
habitat. Researchers are here tagging a
young tiger shark before releasing it so as to
monitor its future movements.

During courtship, male sharks of many species are known to use their teeth to grasp the female behind the first dorsal fin. This female tiger shark bears scars as evidence of this practice. As protection, female sharks often have thicker skin in this region than males of the same species.

Tiger sharks are typified by their huge bulk,
colored gray-green above and white below.
They are circumtropical fish, found both in
coastal and offshore seas and occurring from
the surf line to waters about 460 feet deep.

Tiger sharks have unusually wide mouths, containing rows of large, asymmetrical and saw-edged teeth, resembling cockscombs in overall shape. These are not normally visible until the shark attacks. This particular tiger shark is host to a parasitic copepod in the corner of its mouth.

BLUE SHARK

The blue shark is one of the more slender species and is distinguished by a first dorsal fin that lies well behind the long, narrow pectorals. It is one of the most widespread of all sharks, occurring circumglobally in both temperate and tropical seas.

Blue sharks, also known as bluedogs or blue whalers, have long, conical snouts with the mouth positioned well behind the large eyes. The maximum recorded length for a blue shark is twelve and a half feet.

The blue shark is an appropriately named species since its dorsal surface, fins and tail are a bright indigo blue that contrasts markedly with its white belly. Known as countershading, such coloration is a common feature of pelagic fish, rendering them less visible to predators when seen either from above, against a dark background, or from below, against the light.

The Atlantic sharpnose is, as its name suggests, a shark of the northwest Atlantic Ocean and also of the Caribbean Sea, frequenting, often in large numbers, shallow coastal waters and estuaries. It is also able to enter fresh water, but never ventures far from the sea.

Despite being a requiem shark, the Atlantic sharpnose is of modest proportions, attaining a maximum length of a little over three feet. A broad, flat snout and large eyes are distinctive features of this small, harmless shark.

A surface-dwelling species of the open
ocean, the blue shark pursues its piscine prey
at speeds of up to forty miles an hour.

The timid, largely nocturnal whitetip reef shark is distinguished by the conspicuous white markings on the extremities of all its fins. This six-and-a-half-foot-long shark is found in the tropical Indian and Pacific Oceans, often around coral reefs, at depths ranging from twenty-six to 130 feet. The whitetip is primarily a fish-feeder, and uses its extremely short, broad snout to extract its prey from reef crevices.

Scalloped hammerheads are found
throughout the world in all seas except the
very coldest. This is the commonest of the
hammerheads, and it reaches a maximum
length of over thirteen feet. During the day
scalloped hammerheads often congregate in
schools of about a hundred, dispersing at
night to feed singly. It is not yet known
whether the schools are associated with
mating or social behaviour or whether they
serve as protection against even larger fish.

Adaptation to life on the sea floor has
resulted in a remarkable resemblance
between the angelshark and another
cartilaginous species called the guitarfish,
which is in fact a ray. One clear distinction
between the two is that the angelshark's
head is clearly separated from the front
edges of the pectoral fins, whereas the
outline is continuous in rays.

This Japanese bullhead shark, a species
confined to the northwest Pacific, has been
caught by a diver for tagging. All eight
members of the family Heterodontidae
possess a sharp spine in front of each dorsal
fin and have pronounced ridges above the
eyes. The females produce screw-shaped egg
cases, which are wedged into crevices for
protection against predators.

The horn shark is found in shallow waters in the eastern Pacific. The generic name Heterodontus refers to the fact that these small, blunt-headed sharks possess both biting and crushing teeth, the latter enabling horn sharks to exploit the abundant local supply of tough-shelled benthic molluscs.

The ornate wobbegong is a bottom-dwelling
shark of the western Pacific that is
particularly common in Australian waters. It
reaches a maximum length of some ten feet
and, like all wobbegongs, has powerful jaws
lined with several rows of sharply pointed
teeth, which make it dangerous if provoked.

Wobbegongs have intricately patterned
dorsal surfaces which allow them to remain
undetected as they lie in ambush for the
small fish, shrimps, crabs and other
invertebrates that make up their diet.

Nurse sharks are a sluggish inshore species
found in shallow water in most tropical seas.
In the Atlantic they can be easily
distinguished from all other sharks by the
presence of two barbels on the underside of
the snout. These are probably used for
tactile identification of prey.

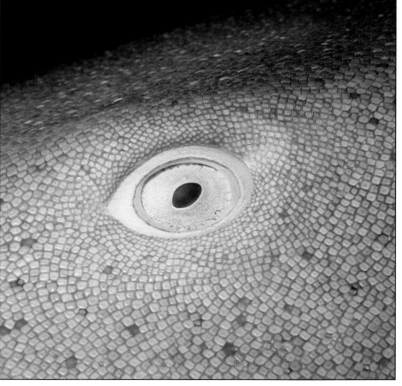

The eyes of sharks are essentially similar to those of all vertebrates; they have two types of light receivers: rods and cones. This means that, in theory, they have both daytime and night-time vision and may even be able to detect color. It is probable, however, that sluggish, shallow-water species, such as the nurse shark, whose eye is shown above, have less acute vision than the active, predatory open-ocean sharks.

Unlike most sharks, which need to keep
swimming to pass water through their gills
to obtain oxygen, nurse sharks are able to lie
motionless on the sea bottom and pump
water over their gills by opening and closing
their mouths. During the day, nurse sharks
are sometimes found piled in underwater
caves in untidy heaps comprising several
dozen individuals.

Nurse sharks and their close relatives have a unique manner of feeding that involves literally sucking their prey into their huge mouth cavities. They are generally an unaggressive species but, if provoked, they can inflict serious wounds with their small but razor-sharp teeth.

The University of Miami has been studying sharks in the wild for many years. Below: researchers inject a tiger shark with tetracycline; this does not harm the shark but provides a wealth of information about the pattern and rate of its growth.

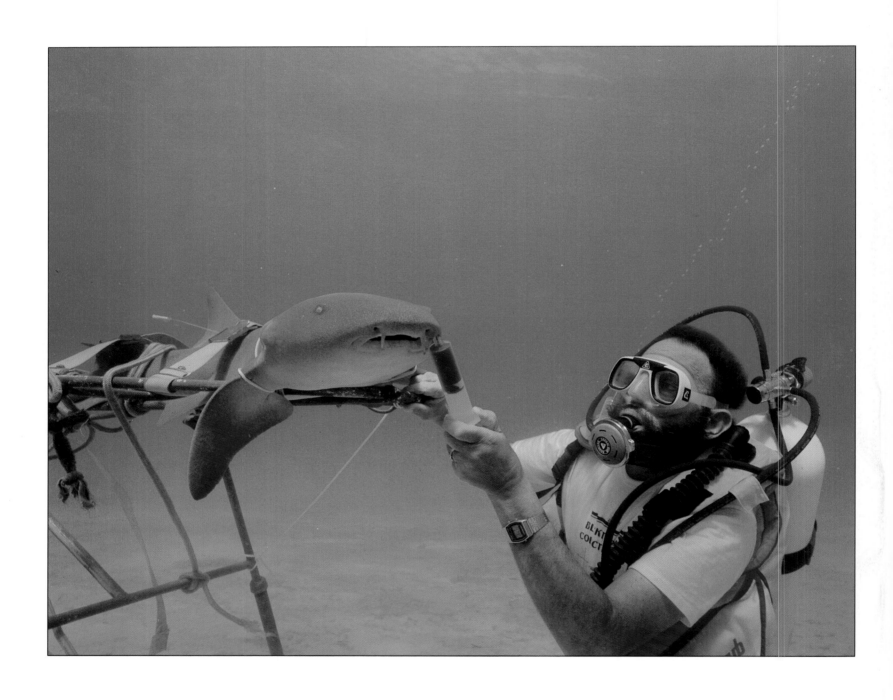

Dr Samuel H. Gruber of the University of
Miami, one of the leading figures in shark
biology and conservation, investigates the
flow of water through the olfactory system of
a nurse shark using a harmless dye.

Having been captured, this great hammerhead shark is being examined for its suitability as a study specimen. Wherever possible, sharks are not removed from the water as the lack of support for their tissues could lead to damage of the vital organs.

Shark reproduction was poorly understood for many years, but the increasing willingness of researchers to take to the water to study their subject has vastly increased knowledge in this field. The capture of a gravid female lemon shark just prior to her giving birth has resulted in a unique photographic record of the delivery.

Pristiophorus japonicus	Japanese sawshark
Pristiophorus nudipinnis	shortnose sawshark
Pristiophorus schroederi	Bahamas sawshark

Superorder: SQUATINOMORPHII

Order: SQUATINIFORMES (angelsharks)

Family: SQUATINIDAE (angelsharks, sand devils)

Squatina aculeata	sawback angelshark
Squatina africana	African angelshark
Squatina argentina	Argentine angelshark
Squatina australis	Australian angelshark
Squatina californica	Pacific angelshark
Squatina dumeril	Atlantic angelshark, sand devil
Squatina formosa	Taiwan angelshark
Squatina japonica	Japanese angelshark
Squatina nebulosa	clouded angelshark
Squatina oculata	smoothback angelshark
Squatina squatina	monkfish, angelshark
Squatina tergocellata	ornate angelshark
Squatina tergocellatoides	ocellated angelshark

Superorder: GALEOMORPHII
Order: HETERODONTIFORMES (bullhead sharks)

Family: HETERODONTIDAE (bullhead sharks, horn sharks)

Heterodontus francisci	horn shark
Heterodontus galeatus	crested bullhead shark
Heterodontus japonicus	Japanese bullhead shark
Heterodontus mexicanus	Mexican hornshark
Heterodontus portusjacksoni	Port Jackson shark
Heterodontus quoyi	Galapagos bullhead shark
Heterodontus ramalheira	whitespotted bullhead shark
Heterodontus zebra	zebra bullhead shark

Order: ORECTOLOBIFORMES (carpetsharks)

Family: PARASCYLLIDAE (collared carpetsharks)

Ciroscyllium expolitum	barbelthroat carpetshark
Ciroscyllium formosanum	Taiwan saddled carpetshark
Ciroscyllium japonicum	saddled carpetshark
Parascyllium collare	collared carpetshark
Parascyllium ferrugineum	rusty carpetshark
Parascyllium multimaculatum	Tasmanian carpetshark
Parascyllium variolatum	necklace carpetshark

Family: BRACHAELURIDAE (blind sharks)
Brachaelurus waddi	blind shark

Family: ORECTOLOBIDAE (wobbegongs)

Eucrossorhinus dasypogon	tasselled wobbegong
Orectolobus japonicus	Japanese wobbegong
Orectolobus maculatus	spotted wobbegong
Orectolobus ornatus	ornate wobbegong
Orectolobus wardi	Northern wobbegong
Sutorectus tentaculatus	cobbler wobbegong

Family: HEMISCYLLIDAE (longtailed carpetsharks, bamboo sharks)

Chiloscyllium arabicum	Arabian carpetshark
Chiloscyllium burmensis	Burmese bambooshark
Chiloscyllium griseum	gray bambooshark
Chiloscyllium hasselti	Indonesian bambooshark
Chiloscyllium indicum	slender bambooshark
Chiloscyllium plagiosum	whitespotted bambooshark
Chiloscyllium punctatum	brownbanded bambooshark
Hemiscyllium freycineti	Indonesian speckled carpetshark
Hemiscyllium hallstromi	Papuan epaulette shark
Hemiscyllium ocellatum	epaulette shark
Hemiscyllium strahani	hooded carpetshark
Hemiscyllium trispeculare	speckled carpetshark

Family: RHINIODONTIDAE (whale sharks, zebra sharks nurse sharks)

Ginglymostoma cirratum	nurse shark
Pseudoginglymostoma brevicaudatum	shorttail nurse shark
Nebrius ferrugineus	tawny nurse or giant sleepy shark
Stegostoma fasciatum	zebra shark
Rhiniodon typus	whale shark

Order: LAMNIFORMES (mackerel sharks)

Family: ODONTASPIDIDAE (sand tiger sharks)

Eugomphodus taurus	sand tiger, spotted raggedtooth, gray nurse shark
Eugomphodus tricuspidatus	Indian sand tiger
Odontaspis ferox	smalltooth sand tiger, bumpytail raggedtooth
Odontaspis noronhai	bigeye sand tiger

Family: MITSUKURINIDAE (goblin sharks)
Mitsukurina owstoni	goblin shark

Family: PSEUDOCARCHARIIDAE (crocodile sharks)
Pseudocarcharias kamoharai	crocodile shark

Family: MEGACHASMIDAE (megamouth sharks)
Megachasma pelagios	megamouth shark

Family: ALOPIIDAE (thresher sharks)
Alopias pelagicus	pelagic thresher
Alopias superciliosus	bigeye thresher
Alopias vulpinus	thresher shark

Family: CETORHINIDAE (basking sharks)
Cetorhinus maximus	basking shark

Family: LAMNIDAE (mackerel sharks)
Carcharodon carcharias	great white shark, maneater, white death
Isurus oxyrinchus	shortfin mako
Isurus paucus	longfin mako
Lamna ditropis	Pacific porbeagle, salmon shark
Lamna nasus	porbeagle, mackerel shark

Order: CARCHARHINIFORMES (ground sharks)
Family: SCYLIORHINIDAE (catsharks)

Apristurus abbreviatus	bignose catshark
Apristurus acanutus	flatnose catshark
Apristurus atlanticus	Atlantic ghost catshark
Apristurus brevicaudatus	
Apristurus brunneus	brown catshark
Apristurus canutus	hoary catshark
Apristurus federovi	Federov's catshark
Apristurus gibbosus	
Apristurus herklotsi	longfin catshark
Apristurus indicus	smallbelly catshark
Apristurus investigatoris	broadnose catshark
Apristurus japonicus	Japanese catshark
Apristurus kampae	longnose catshark
Apristurus laurussoni	Iceland catshark
Apristurus longianalis	
Apristurus longicaudatus	
Apristurus longicephalus	longhead catshark
Apristurus macrorhynchus	flathead catshark
Apristurus macrostomus	
Apristurus maderensis	Madeira catshark
Apristurus manis	ghost catshark
Apristurus microps	smalleye catshark
Apristurus micropterygeus	small dorsal catshark
Apristurus nasutus	largenose catshark
Apristurus parvipinnis	smallfin catshark
Apristurus pinguis	fat catshark
Apristurus platyrhynchus	spatulasnout catshark
Apristurus profundorum	deepwater catshark
Apristurus riveri	broadgill catshark
Apristurus saldanha	Saldanha catshark
Apristurus sibogae	pale catshark
Apristurus sinensis	South China catshark
Apristurus spongiceps	spongehead catshark
Apristurus stenseni	Panama ghost catshark
Apristurus verweyi	Borneo catshark
Apristurus xenolepis	oddscale catshark
Asymbolus analis	Australian spotted catshark
Asymbolus vincenti	Gulf catshark
Atelomycterus mackleayi	Australian marbled catshark
Atelomycterus marmoratus	coral catshark
Aulohalaelurus labiosus	blackspotted catshark
Cephaloscyllium fasciatum	reticulated swellshark
Cephaloscyllium isabellum	draughtsboard shark
Cephaloscyllium laticeps	Australian swellshark
Cephaloscyllium nascione	whitefinned swellshark
Cephaloscyllium silasi	Indian swellshark
Cephaloscyllium sufflans	balloon shark
Cephaloscyllium ventriosum	swellshark
Cephalurus cephalus	lollipop catshark
Galeus arae	roughtail catshark
Galeus boardmani	Australian sawtail catshark
Galeus eastmani	gecko catshark
Galeus longirostris	longnose sawtail catshark
Galeus melastomus	blackmouth catshark

Galeus murinus	mouse catshark
Galeus nipponensis	broadfin sawtail catshark
Galeus piperatus	peppered catshark
Galeus polli	African sawtail catshark
Galeus sauteri	blacktip sawtail catshark
Galeus schultzi	dwarf sawtail catshark
Halaelurus alcocki	Arabian catshark
Halaelurus boesemani	speckled catshark
Halaelurus buergeri	blackspotted catshark
Halaelurus canescens	dusky catshark
Halaelurus clevai	broadhead catshark
Halaelurus dawsoni	New Zealand catshark
Halaelurus hispidus	bristly catshark
Halaelurus immaculatus	spotless catshark
Halaelurus lineatus	lined catshark
Halaelurus lutarius	mud catshark
Halaelurus natalensis	tiger catshark
Halaelurus quagga	quagga catshark
Haploblepharus edwardsii	puffadder shyshark
Haploblepharus fuscus	brown shyshark
Haploblepharus pictus	dark shyshark
Holohalaelurus punctatus	African spotted catshark
Holohalaelurus regani	Izak catshark
Parmaturus campechiensis	Campeche catshark
Parmaturus macmillani	New Zealand filetail
Parmaturus melanobranchius	blackgill catshark
Parmaturus pilosus	salamander shark
Parmaturus xaniurus	filetail catshark
Pentanchus profundicolus	onefin catshark
Poroderma africanum	striped catshark, pyjama shark
Poroderma marleyi	barbeled catshark
Poroderma pantherinum	leopard catshark
Schroederichthys bivius	narrowmouth catshark
Schroederichthys chilensis	redspotted catshark
Schroederichthys maculatus	narrowtail catshark
Schroederichthys tenuis	slender catshark
Scyliorhinus besnardi	polkadot catshark
Scyliorhinus boa	boa catshark
Scyliorhinus caniculus	smallspotted catshark
Scyliorhinus capensis	yellowspotted catshark
Scyliorhinus cervigoni	West African catshark
Scyliorhinus garmani	brownspotted catshark
Scyliorhinus haeckelii	freckled catshark
Scyliorhinus hesperius	whitesaddled catshark
Scyliorhinus meadi	blotched catshark
Scyliorhinus retifer	chain catshark
Scyliorhinus stellaris	nursehound
Scyliorhinus torazame	cloudy catshark
Scyliorhinus torrei	dwarf catshark

Family: PROSCYLLIIDAE (finback catsharks)

Ctenacis fehlmanni	harlequin catshark
Eridacnis barbouri	Cuban ribbontail catshark
Eridacnis radcliffei	pygmy ribbontail catshark
Eridacnis sinuans	African ribbontail catshark
Gollum attenuatus	slender smoothhound

Proscyllium habereri   graceful catshark

Family: PSEUDOTRIAKIDAE (false catsharks)

Pseudotriakis microdon   false catshark

Family: LEPTOCHARIIDAE (barbeled houndsharks)

Leptocharias smithii   barbeled houndshark

Family: TRIAKIDAE (houndsharks)

Furgaleus macki   whiskery shark
Galeorhinus galeus   school shark, tope shark, soupfin shark
Gogolia filewoodi   sailback houndshark
Hemitriakis japanica   Japanese topeshark
Hemitriakis leucoperiptera   whitefin topeshark
Hypogaleus hyugaensis   blacktip topeshark
Iago garricki   longnose houndshark
Iago omanensis   bigeye houndshark
Mustelus antarcticus   gummy shark
Mustelus asterias   starry smoothhound
Mustelus californicus   gray smoothhound
Mustelus canis   dusky smoothhound
Mustelus dorsalis   sharptooth or sharpnose smoothhound
Mustelus fasciatus   striped smoothhound
Mustelus griseus   spotless smoothhound
Mustelus henlei   brown smoothhound
Mustelus higmani   smalleye smoothhound
Mustelus lenticulatus   spotted estuary smoothhound, rig
Mustelus lunulatus   sicklefin smoothhound
Mustelus manazo   starspotted smoothhound
Mustelus mento   speckled smoothhound
Mustelus mosis   Arabian, hardnose or Moses smoothhound
Mustelus mustelus   smoothhound
Mustelus norrisi   narrowfin smoothhound or Florida dogfish
Mustelus palumbes   whitespot smoothhound
Mustelus punctulatus   blackspot smoothhound
Mustelus schmitti   narrownose smoothhound
Mustelus whitneyi   humpback smoothhound
Scylliogaleus quecketti   flapnose houndshark
Triakis acutipinna   sharpfin houndshark
Triakis maculata   spotted houndshark
Triakis megalopterus   sharptooth houndshark or spotted gully shark
Triakis scyllium   banded houndshark
Triakis semifasciata   leopard shark

Family: HEMIGALEIDAE (weasel sharks)

Chaenogaleus macrostoma   hooktooth shark
Hemigaleus microstoma   sicklefin weasel shark
Hemipristis elongatus   snaggletooth shark
Paragaleus leucolomatus   whitetip weasel shark
Paragaleus pectoralis   Atlantic weasel shark
Paragaleus tengi   straighttooth weasel shark

Family: CARCHARHINIDAE (requiem sharks)

Carcharhinus acronotus   blacknose shark
Carcharhinus albimarginatus   silvertip shark

Carcharhinus altimus   bignose shark
Carcharhinus amblyrhynchoides   graceful shark
Carcharhinus amblyrhynchos   gray reef shark
Carcharhinus amboinensis   pigeye or Java shark
Carcharhinus borneensis   Borneo shark
Carcharhinus brachyurus   copper shark or bronze whaler
Carcharhinus brevipinna   spinner shark
Carcharhinus cautus   nervous shark
Carcharhinus dussumieri   whitecheek shark
Carcharhinus falciformis   silky shark
Carcharhinus fitzroyensis   creek whaler
Carcharhinus galapagensis   Galapagos shark
Carcharhinus hemiodon   Pondicherry shark
Carcharhinus isodon   finetooth shark
Carcharhinus leucas   bull, Nicaragua or Zambesi shark
Carcharhinus limbatus   blacktip shark
Carcharhinus longimanus   oceanic whitetip shark
Carcharhinus macloti   hardnose shark
Carcharhinus melanopterus   blacktip reef shark
Carcharhinus obscurus   dusky shark
Carcharhinus perezi   Caribbean reef shark
Carcharhinus plumbeus   sandbar shark
Carcharhinus porosus   smalltail shark
Carcharhinus sealei   blackspot shark
Carcharhinus signatus   night shark
Carcharhinus sorrah   spottail shark
Carcharhinus wheeleri   blacktail reef shark
Galeocerdo cuvier   tiger shark
Glyphis gangeticus   Ganges shark
Glyphis glyphis   speartooth shark
Isogomphodon oxyrhynchus   daggernose shark
Lamiopsis temmincki   broadfin shark
Loxodon macrorhinus   sliteye shark
Nasolamia velox   whitenose shark
Negaprion acutidens   sharptooth lemon shark
Negaprion brevirostris   lemon shark
Prionace glauca   blue shark, blue whaler
Rhizoprionodon acutus   milk shark
Rhizoprionodon lalandii   Brazilian sharpnose shark
Rhizoprionodon longurio   Pacific sharpnose shark
Rhizoprionodon oligolinx   gray sharpnose shark
Rhizoprionodon porosus   Caribbean sharpnose shark
Rhizoprionodon taylori   Australian sharpnose shark
Rhizoprionodon terraenovae   Atlantic sharpnose shark
Scoliodon laticaudus   spadenose shark
Triaenodon obesus   whitetip reef shark

Family: SPHYRNIDAE (hammerhead sharks)

Eusphyra blochii   winghead shark
Sphyrna corona   mallethead shark
Sphyrna lewini   scalloped hammerhead
Sphyrna media   scoophead shark
Sphyrna mokarran   great hammerhead
Sphyrna tiburo   shovelhead shark or bonnethead shark
Sphyrna tudes   smalleye hammerhead
Sphyrna zygaena   smooth hammerhead, balance fish

PICTURE CREDITS

Photographs drawn from the files of Planet Earth Pictures Ltd.
Kurt Amsler: 51, 55; Pete Atkinson: 68; Gaetano Cafiero: 154;
Rosemary Chastney/Ocean Images: 21, 30-31; Dick Clarke: 131;
Walt Clayton/Ocean Images: 25; Martin Coleman: 126; Mark
Conlin: 42, 45, 95, 96, 98-99, 101, 104; Walter Deas: 20, 124, 127;
Alex Double: 116, 117, 123, 136-137; Rodney Fox: 1; David
George: 46; Al Giddings/Ocean Images: 24, 26-27, 28, 32, 64-65,
108, 114; F. Jack Jackson: 50, 54; R.H. Johnson: 69; Robert Jureit:
146, 147; Terry Kerby: 152-153; A. Kerstitch: 43, 44; Ken Lucas:
41, 120, 118, 121, 125, 129; Ned Middleton: 134; Charles
Nicklin/Ocean Images: 22, 35; Doug Perrine: 3, 60-61, 62, 63, 70,
71, 72, 73, 76, 77, 78-79, 80, 81, 82, 83, 86, 87, 88, 89, 90-91, 106-
107, 112, 113, 115, 116-117, 119, 128, 142, 143, 144, 145, 155;
Brian Pitkin: 140, 141; Linda Pitkin: 47; Carl Roessler: 34, 133,
135, 151; Rod Salm: 132; Flip Schulke: 23, 33; Marty Snyderman:
29, 36-37, 40, 84-85, 92-93, 100, 102, 105, 110, 111, 122, 138-139;
Herewarth Voigtmann: 52-53, 56-57, 58-59, 130, 148, 149, 150;
James D. Walt: 4, 48-49, 66, 67, 74, 75; Doc White/Ocean
Images: 109; Warren Williams: 94; Norbert Wu: 38-39, 97, 103.